T°

PURE
FEW
HEARTS

Russ
Rankin

$T°$

THERA BOOKS
Sacramento, California
SAY / SOMETHING

Pure Few Hearts: Poems 1998-2006
Copyright © 2023 by Russ Rankin

Cover photograph by Mark Beemer

Author photograph by Lindsey Lutts McGuire

Cover design by Mona Z. Kraculdy

www.thetherabooks.com

ISBN: 979-8-9863098-2-8
Library of Congress Control Number: 2023932226

A Thera Books First Edition, March 2023

Printed in the United States of America

For my parents,
who would have been stoked to see this happen.

"Russ Rankin's volume of poetry, <u>Pure Few Hearts</u>, slices into the fabric of emotion and psyche. Poem by poem, Rankin's reflections, confessions, and admissions, propel the reader through forms of consciousness oscillating between vulnerability and resilience, sensitivity and intensity, introspection and spontaneity, gathering energy as they navigate landscapes both external and internal. And within this movement is a tone harmonious and dissonant, emerging not only from the language itself but from the urban imagery that Rankin navigates, day after day, week after week, on a road, literal and metaphorical, that seems to never end. Yet when this road does end, the closure of this volume haunts, like the final note of a song ringing out over a crowd slowly exiting a venue, as the band stands on stage, awaiting the inevitable."

—Theodore Shank, author of <u>Follow the Flickering Down</u>

CONTENTS

Santa Monica 1

Don't Go 2

A Studio Breathes 3

Laramie 4

Feels Like Tour 5

Her Bed 6

Familiar 7

Summer 8

Sweet as You Are 9

Hot Coffee 10

Sin City 11

Two Nights Ago 12

Celebrity 13

Hot Country 14

Small World 15

Pointless 16

Pieces 17

Nobody's Hero 18

White Lines 19

Afternoon 20

All American Mating Call 21

Couch 22

Three Girls 24

Vacant 25
Ska Bands 27
Why Do You Perform? 28
Heartful Thoughts 29
Dead Summer Heat 30
Pack It In 32
Highbury 33
Yanks are Coming 34
Bank Holiday 35
Douanes 36
My Finest Hour 37
Amsterdam 38
Continent 39
Marianse 40
We Are a Circus 41
Your New God 42
Graffiti 43
Getting Off Easy 44
And Always the Dogs 45
She'll Be Home 46
Every Third Frame 47
Streetcar Eyes 49
Things Familiar 50
Stripped Away 51
Club Soda 52

Hateful Charade 53
A Strange Beast 54
True Hurt 56
Star Struck 58
Busy? 60
She Could Be 61
Pure Few Hearts 62
Intoxication 63
Human Fragment 64
Borrowed Walls 65
She is Here 67
Relegated 68
Dusk in Surrey 69
Sasketchewan 70
Blank Pages 71
Pachinko 72
A Handful of Days 73
Vain Experiment 74
Worth Her Time 75
As She Smiles 76
In Our Beds 77

Acknowledgments 78

About the Author 79

"Everyone gets everything he wants.
I wanted a mission, and, for my sins, they gave me one.
Brought it up to me like room service.
It was a real choice mission, and, when it was over,
I'd never want another."
—Captain Willard, <u>Apocalypse Now</u>

SANTA MONICA

the midsummer day emerges clear and blue
i am at the santa monica mall
with mother brother cousins and aunt
i buy kiss "alive"
i watch "grease"
i am ten or eleven
later i will drink a can of pepsi light
watch TV and go to sleep
awakening the next morning
to my aunt's call
"olly olly oxen free!"
sour cream pancakes
another slow summer day
swimming in the neighbor's pool
visiting the la brea tar pits
thanking god
that i can't see what's coming

DON'T GO

the way she smells after she's showered
the way her hips sway as she walks
the way her hand feels
clasped in mine
my right her left
her insatiable lust for new shoes
her gestures of playful outrage
when i grab her ass in public
her enchanting southern ontario accent
the way she squints at the television
before or after her contacts are in or out
the way she pouts her lips
stares up at me sadly and says
"don't go"
it is amazing that i manage to go anywhere
with her looking at me that way

russ rankin

A STUDIO BREATHES

a band from michigan
just finishing their record
we're ready to start ours
open front doors
welcome the crisp colorado air
the late afternoon sun glistens
on the dirty sidewalk snow
new drum heads stretched and beaten
sabbath on the tape deck
paranoid
cymbal crashes interspersed
with drum talk i don't understand
days and nights
melt together
unknowingly
without windows
this studio still breathes

LARAMIE

stygian
foreboding
wyoming night
low clouds casting
a dull silver glow
the wind howls
pushes us around
midnight mountains
loom like an alien landscape
the haunted night
illuminated by violent bursts of lightning
left
then right
then dead ahead
momentary brilliance explodes
then back to the darkness
laramie opens up
an oasis of a thousand lights
then it's behind us
and the lights recede
into the cold black night

russ rankin

FEELS LIKE TOUR

today it finally felt like tour
hour after hour in the van
out of books
exhausted
yet unable to sleep
worn eyes limping
to keep up with the speeding scenery
shuffling like the undead
through mini marts and gas stations
growing weary
of the tired teasing
and inane banter
trying to slow the breathing
heart rate
the new coma
eyes closed
practically begging
for even a stitch of sleep
but not today

HER BED

we lie together in her bed
we haven't slept yet
she asks if this is okay with me
"yes"
we kiss for a while
she doesn't really know how
it is both awkward and cute
well into her twenties
she is still a virgin
though she claims somebody i know
tried to rape her once
she tells me i have no idea
how she feels about me
i assure her that i am nothing special
she disagrees

FAMILIAR

two am truck stop neon
buzzing over mississippi insect breeze
could swear i have been here before
so familiar
except that i remember the candy aisle
being much closer to
the nascar merchandise
there is a subway inside
smells like mustard
cigarettes
and fuel
the woman with brown teeth
stares blankly past me as i pay

SUMMER

the sights and sounds of summer
lazy warm breezes
bugs fly unfettered
cars cruise loudly
down small town streets
first band plays
before the sun fades
we move through so many nights
this way
temporary residents
in far too many towns
another day concludes out here
and we are miles from home

russ rankin

SWEET AS YOU ARE

i need to come clean
reel myself in
i haven't been without her
even a minute in my heart
i've had the best intentions
of somehow moving on
i have lent my body out
made a game effort
but sweet as you are
you are not her
and the day may arrive
where that no longer matters
but it hasn't yet

HOT COFFEE

the vehicle lurches then brakes
we file out still half asleep
brushing teeth
showering
some go have a smoke
i want coffee
hot and bracing
we mill about in the decay
read graffiti we've read countless times before
consult the day's proposed schedule
of mind bending tedium
i am like the others
and it sickens me
because I used to think I was different
and was doing something of importance
but it's a joke
a lie
i'm surviving on little sleep
stale bread
and coffee
hot and bracing

russ rankin

SIN CITY

las vegas
the twenty four hour march
of the soulless
americana double wide
over eating over drinking
atm zombies
blank glassy stares
tethered to the slots
bright lights and banging bells
as the money flushes away
slumped over green tables
halos of smoke and indifference
waist deep in the discharge
of baited expectations
and shattered dreams
the husk of our culture
an ironic facade
lit up in neon
the fertile collapse
masked by the glitter
beneath which we suffocate

TWO NIGHTS AGO

i felt it two nights ago
a buzzing sort of itch
like the tail end
of a substandard acid trip
it began in my legs
inside the bones
then to my forehead
behind my tired eyes
in front of my brain
i'm all fucked up
too tired to sleep
and that buzzing
pulsing itch
colors my worrisome dreams
with spiteful decorum

russ rankin

CELEBRITY

a group of eight or nine young people
crowd around the big window
faces and hands pressed against the dark glass
hoping to catch a glimpse of someone
they do not know
convinced that seeing this person
will bring them a moment or two
of fleeting happiness
the seductive qualities of celebrity
are difficult to ascertain
we are all too easily amused
and we tend to gauge our self worth
by our immediate proximity to those
whom we have been trained to adore

HOT COUNTRY

this is the hot country
raising a hand to wipe away sweat
only brings more
every breath of air weighs a ton
even the smallest movement
feels like the hardest thing
you will ever do
fatigue sits perched nearby
he is the vulture
when he comes for me
i will kiss him
and thank him for the relief

russ rankin

SMALL WORLD

a bunch of us are hanging out
st. petersburg parking lot after the show
a ragged woman staggers up to us
she has a filthy t-shirt
and cut off shorts hanging from her spindly frame
"gimme some money"
nobody replies
"gimme a lousy motherfucking dollar"
"we're on tour we don't have any money"
"gimme a cigarette - something!"
someone gives her a beer
she wanders off
now it's the next night
and we're in pensacola

POINTLESS

why should i be honest
when so many around me
lie without conscience?
why should i strive to respect
those whom my companions
objectify and abuse
with crass deliberation?
why should i care
about the trials of the world
when so many blind themselves
with the convenience
of conditional apathy?
why should i attempt
to better myself
when everywhere i look
i see our species devolving?
why should i delve into logic
or reason
when more and more
the world clings
to superficial idolatry
and a culture based on greed?

russ rankin

PIECES

how many others
have stood on this stage?
left sweat and spit?
sometimes i wonder
if i look hard enough
would i find remnants
pieces of me
of my soul
scattered across this stage?
can you see them fall off of me?
every night i come apart
somehow it entertains you
just keep your distance later
when i try to put myself back together
others are waiting for me
to do it all over again
tomorrow night

NOBODY'S HERO

i am nobody's hero
despite what you've heard
i am the walking dead
human emotions are foreign to me
i am a million miles from normal
my thoughts could block out the sun
darken the entire world
to look up to me
is to look down on yourself
i am a one man bad crowd
i am the hangover that never leaves
i am the black cloud
you can't get out from under
the footsteps behind you at night
give me the chance
and i'll sink your ship
leaving you stranded
far from home

russ rankin

WHITE LINES

night drive therapy
thoughts sorted out
ideas fly by
like the mile markers and trees
a chance to reflect
filtering the sanity
out of a twisted existence
the others sleep
i am alone with the frigid night
white lines and truckers
this is the real existence
some say it's crazy
the endless drives
the hours of waiting
the loneliness and exhaustion
they may be right
but it's all we know

AFTERNOON

shirts off
bikes and boards
hot sun cool breeze
people sitting drinking iced coffee
writing reading and talking
an old woman across the street
tending her yard
people walk by slowly
no hurry
no worries
the afternoon stretches
seemingly endless

russ rankin

ALL AMERICAN MATING CALL

the blue flame chevy takes off
pure 1950's retro tire squeal
james dean lookalike contest winner
proud of the heads he turns
she is impressed
her cigarette is red at both ends
he wants to live
in a time he never knew
she wants to die
in a cloud of dust

COUCH

there was a couch
in a cluttered room
and there i'd sit
long stretches
hours
looking at the television
but not really watching
my unease boiling
head pounding
certain i'd long outlived
any usefulness to anybody
dully acting out the final throes
of this eclipse of a life
and what exactly was it
which brought me to this state?
no doubt some minor distraction
which under another's
unfettered gaze
would amount to no large consequence
but damn if i didn't just sit there
clouded over

russ rankin

with anger
pain
frustration
through the fall
winter
and frozen spring months

THREE GIRLS

the three girls in the front
screamed when we hit the stage
whenever i got close enough
they grabbed at me
my legs and crotch
then high fived each other
the oldest was maybe fifteen
after the set they waited
to shake my hand
and they each wanted one of my bracelets

russ rankin

VACANT

i float distended
through the time lapse cannonade
of traffic lights stretched
like neon taffy
through a week's worth
of release and transit
the compacted existence
and pastel walls
punctuate the empty manner
in which i drape these days
over me
it is a tangible space
vacant now
that she once filled
and so
my search lumbers on
my will to compete
nearly broken
eyes which have bled
too many silent tears
i move closer

yet remain separate
i am damaged beyond recall
a dry well of hours
days
months
time spent in the naive pursuit
of the life i see
in everyone but me

russ rankin

SKA BANDS

we are on tour with a ska band
their live show is clownish
the kids eat it up
the band encourages the youths
to consume large amounts of alcohol
and remove their clothes onstage
no thank you
i am immediately suspicious
of anything so overtly happy
as these ska bands

WHY DO YOU PERFORM?

the opening band sound checks
doors in an hour
stretch play sweat
obliterate myself
"why do you perform?" she asks
to keep myself from going insane
while at the same time
ensuring that at some point
i will
maybe even tonight

russ rankin

HEARTFUL THOUGHTS

this path i've chosen
is perhaps best travelled alone
i push aside
the heartful thoughts
i wince and pine
i dream self destructively
of the nights with her
in hindsight
i had it all
i envy the lightest touch
and the most arcane affections
between strangers at the traffic light
or in the cinema
it seems everybody but me
has been successfully matched up
sorted compatibly
i wait for mine
with the gnawing fear
growing at the base of my skull
that she has come
and gone
forever

pure few hearts

DEAD SUMMER HEAT

the droning backbeat
of monotony and routine
load ins and load outs
every year the same towns
my tired eyes mist
like a cotton mouth cough
forever it seems i've spent
a transient existence this way
time passes
with the ease of a hyper extended psyche
ever count the stars
on an 80 degree southern night?
ever rend yourself
into a thousand pieces onstage
only to climb tattered behind the wheel
for an eleven hour drive
to do it all over again?
ever feel the sanity and years
peel off of you
with each passing mile?
to lie in this bed

russ rankin

is to be ravaged by exhaustion
and so it goes
in the dead summer heat

PACK IT IN

van keys dangling
jangling
and the studded white belts
and blue jean brawn
black tees tight
under greasy unwashed bangs
what tour has become
i am sad
embarrassed
for all of us
most need to bow out
maybe me too

russ rankin

HIGHBURY

the twilight chill
of highbury park
london at dusk
where the air is thick
with the collective release
of population
their worries
their angst
released into the gray cold
drifting into a friday night
the big red buses
talking them to chelsea
or knightsbridge
or sloan square to piccadilly
the beast is waking
as the week recedes

YANKS ARE COMING

awake in the crumbling remains of the city
foreigners weigh our appearance
with hushed conversations
and train station stares
another day off spent wandering
beneath the indecisive european sky
cold or warm?
rain or not?
i grab my jacket just in case
brush my teeth
splash cold water on my face
we walk the streets
people give us plenty of space
and pull their children close
what a sight we must be
each day out here
takes me further away
from caring what they think of me
we are in the middle of it all
and there is nothing they can do

russ rankin

BANK HOLIDAY

irregular sun
graces this monday morning scene
manchester awakes
to a breezy bank holiday
last time i was here
i wanted to break a bottle
over a kid's head
today?
it's a blank page

DOUANES

clearing customs
douanes
there she is
she's brought a dozen roses
for me
she says laughingly
they're so she might "get lucky"
but that was years ago

MY FINEST HOUR

back here for the first time
since it ended
the scene of the sweetest crime
last night i was at the restaurant
where we went
not five minutes after
she said "yes"
on the moonlit beach
me on one knee
they took our picture
her eyes still glassy from the happy tears
brand new ring
glowing on her finger
as though it had lived there always
the pillars of experience are unforgiving
the dull pain prescient
and the intoxication of that moment
is lost on me now

AMSTERDAM

the assembled crowd cheers
a juggler performs
on a raised unicycle
a near naked man balances
on a suspended rope
the small cup is half full of espresso
that's what they bring you here
when you order a coffee
five guilders
the wind rustles the umbrellas
which say "coca cola"
a blurred montage
of earthy gray coats
wave after wave of dutch people on bikes
bright yellow streetcar
speeds between it all
gray windy sky
drops of rain fall
a million tiny splashes
in the murky green canal

russ rankin

CONTINENT

fell asleep in amsterdam
woke up in hasselt belgium
loaded in
got some coffee
the clouds overhead
lie about the sun
you could forget there was one
if you hung out here long enough
with the gray skies
muddy ground
and crumbling walls

MARIANSE

her name is marianse
black is the color
of her shoes pants shirt and hair
she smokes one cigarette after another
i have known her four hours
we haven't spoken
she has caught me looking at her
several times already
maybe i am creeping her out
but i have decided that i love her
even though she smokes

russ rankin

WE ARE A CIRCUS

concentrating just to keep cool
in the hazy day long wait
middle of nowhere
nothing
i drink coffee
as i gaze out over this mud caked belgian field
we primp and pose
lean into character
we are a circus
and we belong inside these tents

YOUR NEW GOD

in ten years will you still be here?
will you still care?
or will the raised fist of opposition
devolve into the reticent hand of defeat?
will the injustices of the world
still move you?
or will you shut the blinds
turn up the television
and thank your new god
that it's not happening
down your street?

russ rankin

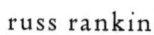

GRAFFITI

two young girls in winter coats
squatting head to head
near a crumbling cinder wall
held together by layers of graffiti
with bright blue plastic shovels
they till the fecund soil
and discuss things of worldly import
to a german girl of five
they dig and talk
talk and dig
on an otherwise barren
windswept street

GETTING OFF EASY

the air is stale and cigarette
the manner is efficient and guttural
hearty bread
room temperature cola
i write each time
and it never changes
one more night
in germany
we got off easy

russ rankin

AND ALWAYS THE DOGS

the rare northern sun
sends a scattered shadow
across the dew specked grass floor
of the open air venue
squatters huddle and smoke
listening to discharge
and always the dogs
the ever present familiars
of the dedicated anti socialites
with their pink dreads
and conflict shirts
tonight strains of empowerment
will ring off the graffiti caked walls
of this former slaughterhouse
while outside
people will be selling french fries and cigarettes

SHE'LL BE HOME

the bearded man
in pastel blue overalls
the aryan princess
with sagging breasts and tar stained teeth
the unwashed stench
of urine vomit and tile
the earthy coffee
which practically dares you to drink it
the hot air tomb
which transports us
the empty listless hours spent waiting
for the appropriate time when
back in a world that's inches
from forgetting you
she'll be home to take your call

EVERY THIRD FRAME

he staggers and weaves
sweaty disheveled
large eyes rolled back
done in on liquor
pills
who knows what else
he fumbles and flails
he is tolerated
propped up
only to pitch forward yet again
he has paid his money
had what for him
passes as fun
he will come to
bruised and foggy
remembering only every third frame
of a hundred shot roll
were i not in the midst
of a performance
i could steal a moment
of compassion

remembering nights
such as his
are what ultimately prevent me
from suffering more of them myself

russ rankin

STREETCAR EYES

I see you for an instant
the fleeting streetcar eyes
and i dash to read your thoughts
our gazes lock
for only a second
can you see
how broken i've become?
a desperate recluse
staring back at you
from yet another smoke filled
coffee house refuge

THINGS FAMILIAR

the evening sun sits poised
to duck behind the rows
of florentine tile roofs
the twisting narrow streets
are lined with tiny french cars
my throat feels like a gravel pit
hygiene is reduced
to a half full bottle of tepid water
poured over my aching head
locked into the plan
i wait
surrounded by this foreign landscape
things familiar
are elusive here
and my swollen eyes watch
as the sun dips lower
my sorrow is measured
by my success
and when i walk
my shadow leads

russ rankin

STRIPPED AWAY

"my god" i wonder
as i slump here
in the dim lights and beer
a snare drum in the next room
now a rack tom
"where is she?
what am i doing here?"
i am mostly stripped away now

CLUB SODA

the white coned walls
reach and beckon
the gray sea chops
with craft and wind
the lucky gull
with a mouthful of fish
three teenage girls
toss a butt into the trash
giggle embarrassed
as it begins to smolder
then smoke
groups of tourists
climb the harbor bridge
and i blink it all away
with club soda and lime

russ rankin

HATEFUL CHARADE

i want to get out
of this band
this life
this hateful charade
i am an insult to myself
by even being here
carrying on
as if there's some token relevance
to any of it
some dramatic twist
which will jar me
into an unforeseen awakening
to remark on how it was all
worth it
and so i wait
feeling foolish in the process

A STRANGE BEAST

why do they bother?
take the time
travel
sometimes extravagant distances
pay their hard earned euros
for the opportunity to gawk
insult
spit
and hurl bottles
it is as if
they relish the opportunity
to hate us as virulently as they love us
an american is a strange beast
an american band
an even stranger one
up there each night
we play our songs
they shout and jeer
we leave puzzled by it all
not exactly sure
what they were doing

russ rankin

only that there were more doing it
than last time

TRUE HURT

i wonder where she is right now
i wonder if she thinks of me at all
we came pretty close
to going all the way
she didn't want it
didn't want me
it would have been great
i wrote songs for her
about her
her name is on my right leg
forever
i still have the promise ring
she wouldn't accept
sometimes even now
when i hear a certain song
or drive by a place
where we spent time together
i start to cry
and my bones ache
will this ever stop?
year after year i struggle

russ rankin

to close the door
on what we had
i swing the door as hard as i can
then rush to stop it
from closing all the way
leaving it open
just an inch or so
because you never know
she may want to come back
and she's lost her key
i've lost my mind
this is the true hurt
it hardens the heart
and makes me keep the next one
that much further away

STAR STRUCK

with pinhole lives
we break this weary canter
surprised
held fast
by the surrogate storm
of flaccid elation
elements composed
of a martyr's sand
relevance pure
yet discounted
we lash out
loud and spitty
unfocused rage
availing itself nothing solid
no remorse
displaced through the everlast
dipping and plunging
a fateful escape
from the high sign madness
revealing the viral link
secondary

awash in the pallid glow
of all the empty hours
star struck
like a vine through time
and i swing wearily
surprised
impressed
disgraced
by less and less

BUSY?

the barricade is up
and the light techs
are busy with the lights
and the sound men
are working on the sound
and yet i am still here
on a sterile concrete bench
inside a musty disco basement
in a crowded italian city
and the smell is effusive
and the day simply refuses to end

russ rankin

SHE COULD BE

the working class goes by
i see them all
through yet another cafe pane
my favorite film
i am lost in it all
with no one to call
or miss
or mark the ardor
of my absence against
yet stubbornly aware
that she could well be
the next living soul
to enter my field of vision

PURE FEW HEARTS

on and on
city by city
rain or shine
we load in
they show up
they sing dance cry
appreciate
numbers up
numbers down
never the most important
yet golden
in the pure few hearts
i wish i could give them more
they are everything to me

russ rankin

INTOXICATION

every single day
i am confronted by opportunities
to poison my mind and body
to momentarily escape
through voluntary ingestion
of one or more chemicals
intoxication
to say it didn't sound inviting
now and then would be a lie
still one more day i politely abstain
opting not to taint my reality
where you see diversion
i see captivity
what you find cool
i find weak
to construct a good time from weakness
holds no appeal for me
i'll limp along without your crutches
and i'll find my truth
in an unpolluted mind

HUMAN FRAGMENT

these tired anxious days
i endeavor to read the guarded minds
of everyone i pass
on the barren streets
six thousand miles
from the minds i know
the talk is loud
and the manner brittle
as if to break at any moment
what then holds it all
us all
in place?
where is the acrimonious glue
and the idyllic adhesive
to our human fragment?

russ rankin

BORROWED WALLS

nights like these
where we borrow the brick walls
sentiments spoken
through cigarette clouds
reconnection
nervously avoiding eye contact
with the omnipotent
impermanence of it all
lacking both the wisdom
and forethought
to savor these moments
of imaginary gravity
of an existence
which will one day play
it's inevitable hand
and wrap its toxic arms around
the shortening hours
and the borrowed walls
will give way to cell block bars
restrained by families and responsibilities
trapped and frail

wishing once more
for these long slow evenings
in the borrowed walls
with cigarette clouds

russ rankin

SHE IS HERE

the girl is here
i hoped she would be
we see each other
she is
expectant?
waiting?
i do not speak
she leaves
and so it goes

RELEGATED

i breathe and walk
but i am not alive
this is routine
and yet it is every bit as abrasive
as the very first time
can it really be eleven years ago?
the techno artist I am listening to
was probably still in grade school
years from cutting their first vocal
while i was cutting myself to pieces
and for what?
where has it all led me?
tonight it's a dingy club
with tattered couches
and a capacity of 375 people

russ rankin

DUSK IN SURREY

it is near dusk in surrey british columbia
for once the sun is warm
birds and airplanes provide the soundtrack
mario's father died today
his family needs him now
more than we do
people dying
others just being born
most of us caught
somewhere in between
got to thinking of my dad
i never see him anymore
it's my fault as much as his
i couldn't imagine him dying
he is and was superman to me
his health should be beyond worry
but it's not

SASKETCHEWAN

the chill is bone deep
the wind howls
hammering the vehicle from all sides
swerving like a drunk
lonely gusting prairie drive
one more sleepless night
another test to pass
i switch to automatic
sleep is now a hindrance
rest is for other people
out here it's real
blinding furious alive
home is one desolate truck stop after another
one bleak nowhere town
like the last one
the freezing wind tries to slow us down
but we persevere
until it's done

russ rankin

BLANK PAGES

when i no longer walk talk
or breathe
when my insides cease to function
will i leave anything substantial?
will anything i have done
said
or erected
during my brief tour here
empower
enlighten
or endure?
when i happen to pause
in the course of an average day
and think these thoughts
it's as if time itself hits me
on its way to wherever
it is going
in such a hurry
there are no answers for me
in this life
only these long days
and blank pages to fill

PACHINKO

lit up like the fourth of july
each neighborhood spilling into the next
lights flash
and the pachinko bells clang
every building animated
these people have never been to detroit
or downtown cincinnati
they may never know how good they have it
but they seem content
as they ought to be

A HANDFUL OF DAYS

days grow shorter
down to single digits
the behemoth tour which had loomed
menacing before us
has withered away
to a handful of days
once more
we've matched wits
with the road
and time has worn on
steadily
just like always

VAIN EXPERIMENT

the shutters shake
from the tooth grind
the subject works to free itself
from the sweat soaked sheet cocoon
the men who breathe indifference
dot the west walls of the room
from trial to vain experiment
to motels on the moon

russ rankin

WORTH HER TIME

each year
each passing day
in the grips of this
i awaken
a bit more deprived
awkward steel moments
more life thrown
mightily into the vastness
and each new morning
offers it's sweet
temporary surrender
from the knowing
and remembering
when i was worth her time

AS SHE SMILES

initials on a sidewalk
a branch falls from a tree
a small stone fountain washes
the hours off of me
a life which measures sideways
the years wear into miles
the solitude surrounds me
i shiver through the trials
our footsteps fade to memories
as she looks back and smiles

russ rankin

IN OUR OWN BEDS

final night of tour
the preceding days dragged
so near the end
yet still so far from home
tonight we will sleep in our own beds
and need no wake up calls
i feel tired and worn
yet content
more uselessness has fallen away
getting closer to the real
peeling away the layers
of what makes me similar to you
exposing the truth and separation
living within the normal boundaries
while at the same time
completely removed from them
torturing myself
in order to break free
of someone else's idea
about whom i should be

Wasted Life Ain't No Crime - 7 Seconds

ACKNOWLEDGMENTS

Massive thanks to Ted Shank, for his aid and guidance throughout the process of curating this collection. His eye for detail, and his ability to steer the work, while maintaining its thematic integrity, were indispensable.

russ rankin

ABOUT THE AUTHOR

Russ Rankin is best known as the singer for punk bands Good Riddance and Only Crime, as well as performing and releasing music as a solo artist. Good Riddance has released, to date, nine full-length albums and an EP, and have toured throughout the world extensively for over two decades. Only Crime has released three full-length albums and has toured extensively throughout the last fifteen years. Rankin released his second full-length solo album in 2022 and has performed throughout North America and Europe. Throughout the 2000s, Rankin held down a monthly column in <u>Amp Magazine</u> while also contributing to publications such as <u>Alternative Press</u>, <u>Razorcake</u>, <u>Warped Tour</u>, <u>Harvest</u>, and <u>New Noise</u>, among others. Rankin later contributed two regular columns to the <u>Washington Times</u> and has contributed to sites such as <u>Punk Guru</u>. Aside from writing and performing music, Rankin also serves as the California scout for the Tri-City Americans of the Western Hockey League. Rankin lives in Santa Cruz, California, with his two cats.

russ rankin

$T°$